A Comprehensive Guide to Medicinal Plants and Their Uses

Raja Sekhar

Published by Raja Sekhar, 2023.

A COMPREHENSIVE GUIDE TO MEDICINAL PLANTS AND THEIR USES

First edition. August 16, 2023.

ISBN: 979-8223504900

Written by Raja Sekhar.

About The Author

RajaSekhar, the accomplished author of "A Comprehensive Guide to Medicinal Plants and Their Uses," possesses an innate passion for the natural world and its healing potential. With an extensive background in botany and a profound interest in herbal remedies, RajaSekhar's journey into the realm of plant-based medicine has been a lifelong pursuit.

Having studied under renowned herbalists and ethno-botanists, RajaSekhar's expertise is rooted in both traditional practices and modern scientific understanding. His dedication to bridging these worlds has resulted in a comprehensive guide that seamlessly weaves together ancient wisdom and contemporary research.

RajaSekhar's genuine reverence for the power of nature's remedies is palpable in his writing. His exploration of medicinal plants and their applications is not merely academic; it's a reflection of his deep belief in the holistic potential of these natural wonders. Through meticulous research and a commitment to accuracy, RajaSekhar imparts a wealth of knowledge to readers eager to explore the healing properties of plants.

As an author, RajaSekhar's mission extends beyond education; it's a call to action. His guide empowers readers to take control of their well-being by harnessing the therapeutic gifts of nature. By demystifying complex botanical concepts, RajaSekhar ensures that readers, from novice to enthusiast, can confidently incorporate herbal remedies into their lives.

RajaSekhar's "A Comprehensive Guide to Medicinal Plants and Their Uses" is a testament to his dedication to holistic health, his respect for the wisdom of traditional practices, and his commitment to providing readers with a reliable resource for understanding and utilizing nature's bounty for wellness. Through his words, RajaSekhar invites us all to embark on a journey of healing, guided by the timeless wisdom of the plant kingdom.

Introduction

Welcome to "A Comprehensive Guide to Medicinal Plants and Their Uses." In this Book, we will explore the fascinating world of medicinal plants and discover the diverse range of natural remedies they offer. For centuries, various cultures have relied on the healing properties of plants to treat ailments, boost overall health, and promote well-being. Through this Book, you will gain insights into the history, benefits, and practical applications of some of the most renowned medicinal plants.

Disclaimer

The information provided in this Book is for educational purposes only and should not be considered as medical advice. Always consult with a healthcare professional before using herbal remedies, especially if you are pregnant, nursing, or taking medications.

Happy reading and may the healing powers of medicinal plants enrich your life!

Contents

Chapter 1: The Art of Herbal Medicine

- Understanding the history and importance of herbal medicine in different cultures.
- Exploring the science behind herbal remedies and the active compounds responsible for their healing effects.
- Understanding the significance of traditional herbal knowledge and the transition to modern herbalism.

Chapter 2: Harvesting and Preparing Medicinal Plants

- Guidelines for responsible and sustainable harvesting of medicinal plants.
- Proper techniques for drying, storing, and preserving herbs to maintain their potency.
- Preparing herbal remedies such as teas, tinctures, infusions, and poultices.

Chapter 3: The Top Medicinal Plants and Their Uses

1. Aloe Vera: Soothing skin ailments, aiding digestion, and promoting wound healing.
2. Ginger: Easing nausea, reducing inflammation, and supporting digestion.
3. Echinacea: Strengthening the immune system and fighting respiratory infections.
4. Chamomile: Calming anxiety, promoting sleep, and soothing digestive discomfort.
5. Turmeric: Anti-inflammatory properties, aiding digestion, and supporting joint health.
6. Peppermint: Relieving headaches, easing indigestion, and alleviating respiratory issues.
7. Lavender: Reducing stress and anxiety, promoting relaxation, and aiding sleep.

8. Garlic: Boosting the immune system, supporting heart health, and fighting infections.
9. Ginkgo Biloba: Enhancing memory and cognitive function, supporting brain health.
10. Calendula: Soothing skin irritations, promoting wound healing, and reducing inflammation.

Chapter 4: Herbal Remedies for Common Ailments
● Herbal treatments for coughs, colds, and flu symptoms.
● Managing digestive issues and promoting gut health with herbal remedies.
● Natural solutions for stress, anxiety, and sleep disturbances.
● Herbal first aid for minor injuries and skin conditions.
Chapter 5: Safety and Precautions
● Understanding potential side effects and interactions with medications.
● Identifying poisonous plants and avoiding accidental ingestion.
● Best practices for consulting healthcare professionals and herbalists when necessary.

Chapter 1: The Art of Herbal Medicine

● Understanding the History and Importance of Herbal Medicine in Different Cultures

Herbal medicine, also known as herbalism or botanical medicine, is one of the oldest healing practices in the world. It has been an integral part of human civilizations for millennia and continues to be cherished and practiced in various cultures worldwide. In this chapter, we will delve into the fascinating history of herbal medicine and explore its enduring significance across different societies.

1. Historical Origins of Herbal Medicine: The roots of herbal medicine can be traced back to ancient civilizations like the Egyptians, Chinese, Greeks, and indigenous cultures. Early humans instinctively sought out plants to address various health concerns, learning through trial and error which plants had beneficial effects and which were harmful. This knowledge was passed down through generations, giving rise to traditional herbal knowledge.

2. Herbal Medicine in Different Cultures: Herbal medicine evolved independently in diverse regions, resulting in unique healing systems. Some notable examples include:

● Traditional Chinese Medicine (TCM): TCM places a strong emphasis on herbal remedies, using hundreds of plants to address imbalances in the body and maintain harmony between yin and yang energies.

● Ayurveda: Originating in India, Ayurveda relies on a wide range of herbs to restore balance in the body's doshas (vata, pitta, kapha) and promote holistic well-being.

● Indigenous Medicine: Various indigenous cultures, such as Native American, Aboriginal, and African tribes, have their own herbal healing traditions based on their local plant resources.

1. The Revival of Herbalism: During the Middle Ages, herbal knowledge flourished in Europe, with monastic gardens serving as repositories of herbal wisdom. However, as modern medicine emerged, the popularity of herbalism waned. In recent times, there has been a resurgence of interest in herbal medicine, driven by a desire for natural remedies and a return to traditional healing practices.

2. The Importance of Traditional Herbal Knowledge: The wealth of traditional herbal knowledge is a testament to the ingenuity and observation skills of ancient healers. Passed down orally or through written texts, this knowledge has been carefully preserved and continues to be a valuable resource for modern herbalists and researchers.

3. Modern Scientific Validation: In recent decades, scientific research has begun to validate the efficacy of many medicinal plants used in traditional herbal medicine. This bridge between ancient wisdom and modern science has led to the incorporation of herbal remedies into mainstream healthcare.

▪ Exploring the Science Behind Herbal Remedies and Their Active Compounds

Herbal remedies have been used for centuries to address various health concerns, and as modern science advances, researchers have sought to uncover the scientific basis behind their healing effects. In this chapter, we will explore the fascinating world of herbal compounds and the scientific evidence supporting their therapeutic properties.

1.   Phytochemicals: The Healing Power of Plants

Plants are abundant sources of diverse chemical compounds known as phytochemicals. These bioactive substances are responsible for the medicinal properties of herbs. Some common phytochemicals include alkaloids, flavonoids, terpenes, phenolic acids, and essential oils. Each phytochemical has unique characteristics and can contribute to specific health benefits.

1.   Pharmacological Actions of Herbal Compounds

Scientific studies have revealed that phytochemicals interact with biological systems, producing pharmacological effects in the body. For example:

- Alkaloids found in plants like poppy and quinine have pain-relieving and anti-inflammatory properties.

- Flavonoids, present in fruits and vegetables, act as antioxidants and help combat oxidative stress.

- Terpenes, found in essential oils, have antimicrobial and anti-inflammatory actions.

- Phenolic acids in plants like green tea have potential anti-cancer and cardiovascular benefits.

1. Synergy and Holistic Effects

One of the most intriguing aspects of herbal medicine is the concept of synergy. In many herbal remedies, the combined action of multiple compounds creates a synergistic effect, enhancing the overall therapeutic benefit. This holistic approach recognizes that the whole plant often works better than isolated compounds alone.

1. Modern Research on Herbal Remedies

Recent scientific studies have explored the efficacy of various herbal remedies. Some examples of well-researched herbal compounds and their uses include:

- Curcumin from turmeric, with potent anti-inflammatory and antioxidant properties.

- Echinacea extracts, which may enhance the immune system and help combat respiratory infections.

- Garlic's active compound allicin, which has shown cardiovascular benefits and potential antimicrobial effects.

- Ginkgo biloba extract, which may improve cognitive function and circulation.

1. Safety and Side Effects

While herbal remedies generally have a good safety profile, it is essential to recognize that some compounds may interact with medications or cause adverse effects in certain individuals. Herbalists and healthcare professionals emphasize the importance of proper dosing and individualized treatments.

● Understanding the Significance of Traditional Herbal Knowledge and the Transition to Modern Herbalism

Traditional herbal knowledge forms the foundation of herbal medicine and has been an essential part of human culture for millennia. Passed down through generations, this wisdom is a valuable repository of the healing properties of plants and their applications. In this chapter, we will explore the significance of traditional herbal knowledge and the evolution of herbalism into the modern era.

1. Wisdom of Ancestral Healing: Traditional herbal knowledge is the accumulated wisdom of our ancestors, gained through centuries of observing and interacting with the natural world. Early humans relied on their keen observation skills and a deep understanding of their environment to identify plants with medicinal properties. They discovered which plants could treat various ailments, alleviate pain, and promote well-being. This knowledge was shared orally and transmitted from elders to the younger generations, preserving the healing traditions of different cultures.

2. Cultural Diversity and Regional Wisdom: Each culture developed its unique herbal knowledge based on the plants available in their geographical region, climate, and ecosystem. Indigenous peoples around the world possess intricate knowledge of local flora and their healing potential. This cultural diversity enriches the collective herbal wisdom, providing a vast array of remedies for addressing health issues.

3. The Role of Healers and Shamans: In traditional societies, healers and shamans were respected members of their communities, serving as guardians of herbal knowledge and medicine. They played a vital role in diagnosing illnesses, administering herbal treatments, and conducting healing

rituals. The knowledge and skills of these healers were deeply ingrained in their cultural practices and often held sacred.

4. Challenges to Traditional Herbalism: As modern medicine and pharmaceuticals emerged, traditional herbalism faced challenges and declined in some societies. The advent of industrialization and urbanization led to a disconnection from nature and a loss of traditional healing practices. In some cases, colonialism and cultural assimilation further eroded the transmission of traditional knowledge.

5. The Transition to Modern Herbalism: Despite the challenges, the value of traditional herbal knowledge persisted and experienced a resurgence in the 20th century. As people sought more natural and holistic approaches to health, interest in herbal medicine grew. Modern herbalism bridges the gap between ancient wisdom and contemporary science. It embraces traditional knowledge while integrating evidence-based research and clinical studies to validate the efficacy and safety of herbal remedies.

6. Herbal Education and Research: Modern herbalists undergo formal education and training in botany, plant identification, pharmacology, and traditional herbal practices. They combine this knowledge with contemporary scientific understanding to create evidence-informed treatment plans for their clients. Additionally, ongoing research in herbal medicine continues to unveil the active compounds and mechanisms of action behind the healing properties of plants.

Chapter 2: Harvesting and Preparing Medicinal Plants

● Guidelines for Responsible and Sustainable Harvesting of Medicinal Plants

Harvesting medicinal plants is a delicate process that requires careful consideration for the preservation of these valuable resources and the ecosystems they inhabit. Irresponsible harvesting practices can lead to the depletion of plant populations and disrupt local ecosystems. In this chapter, we will explore guidelines for responsible and sustainable harvesting of medicinal plants, ensuring their availability for future generations and promoting ecological balance.

1. Understanding Local Regulations: Before embarking on any harvesting activities, it is crucial to familiarize yourself with local, regional, and national regulations related to plant harvesting. Many countries have laws protecting endangered or threatened plant species, and some areas may be designated as protected or sensitive habitats. Adhering to these regulations ensures the preservation of medicinal plants and prevents legal repercussions.

2. Respect for Traditional Territories and Indigenous Knowledge: If harvesting medicinal plants in areas traditionally inhabited by indigenous communities, it is essential to seek permission and guidance from local knowledge holders. Indigenous communities often have deep-rooted relationships with the land and possess valuable insights into sustainable harvesting practices. Respecting their traditions and knowledge fosters a more responsible and culturally sensitive approach to plant harvesting.

3. Identify Abundant and Invasive Species: Focus on harvesting

medicinal plants that are abundant and not at risk of overharvesting. Avoid harvesting rare or threatened species, as well as those that are critical to local ecosystems. In some cases, certain medicinal plants may be invasive species that threaten native flora and fauna. Harvesting these invasive plants can help control their spread and benefit the ecosystem.

4. Practice Selective Harvesting: Adopt a selective harvesting approach, taking only what is needed and leaving the majority of the plant population intact. Avoid uprooting entire plants unless necessary, as this can disrupt the plant's ability to regenerate. Instead, focus on harvesting leaves, flowers, or seeds, depending on the part of the plant used for medicinal purposes.

5. Preserve Seed and Propagate: Consider preserving seeds or propagating medicinal plants in suitable environments. By collecting seeds responsibly and sowing them in controlled settings, you can contribute to the sustainable propagation of the plant species and help maintain genetic diversity.

6. Avoid Harvesting Near Polluted Areas: Medicinal plants can absorb pollutants from their surroundings, potentially compromising their safety and efficacy. Avoid harvesting plants from areas near industrial sites, polluted water sources, or places with heavy pesticide use. Opt for harvesting in pristine environments whenever possible.

7. Ethical and Sustainable Wildcrafting: Wildcrafting refers to the sustainable harvesting of wild plants. If you engage in wildcrafting, do so ethically by respecting the balance of ecosystems. Harvest in moderation, spread out the collection over a wide area, and avoid damaging habitats or disturbing wildlife.

○ Proper techniques for drying, storing, and preserving herbs to maintain their potency

Properly drying, storing, and preserving herbs is crucial to maintain their potency and maximize their shelf life. Improper handling can lead to the loss of essential oils and active compounds, resulting in reduced effectiveness. In this chapter, we will explore the techniques for effectively drying, storing, and preserving herbs to ensure their potency and quality.

1. Drying Herbs:

● Harvest herbs during the morning, after the dew has dried, but before the sun is at its peak. This is when the essential oils are at their highest concentration.

● Choose healthy and mature herb stems without signs of mold or pests. Wash them gently to remove any dirt or debris.

● Bundle small bunches of herbs together and secure them with twine or rubber bands. This allows for better air circulation during drying.

● Hang the herb bundles upside down in a well-ventilated area away from direct sunlight. This can be done indoors or in a shaded, dry outdoor location.

● Ensure that the herbs are fully dried before moving to the next step. They should be crisp and crumble easily when touched.

1. Storing Dried Herbs:

● Once herbs are fully dried, remove the leaves and flowers from the stems. Discard any damaged or discolored parts.

● Store the dried herbs in airtight containers, such as glass jars with tight-fitting lids. Make sure the containers are clean and dry before adding the herbs.

● Label each container with the name of the herb and the date of drying to track freshness.

● Keep the containers in a cool, dark, and dry place. Exposure to light, heat, and moisture can cause the herbs to degrade more quickly.

1.   Preserving Herbs:

● To preserve the potency of dried herbs, avoid crushing or grinding them until you are ready to use them. Whole or coarsely crushed herbs retain their flavor and aroma better.

● Avoid using plastic bags for long-term storage, as they may not provide an airtight seal and can cause condensation.

● If you have an excess of dried herbs, consider making herb-infused oils, vinegars, or herbal teas. These preparations can preserve the flavor and medicinal properties of the herbs for an extended period.

1.   Testing Herb Potency:

● Over time, the potency of herbs may decrease. To test the potency of dried herbs, crush a small amount between your fingers and smell or taste it. If the aroma and flavor are weak, it may be time to replace or refresh your herb supply.

● Preparing herbal remedies such as teas, tinctures, infusions, and poultices

Preparing herbal remedies is an art that allows you to harness the healing properties of medicinal plants. Different methods of preparation, such as teas, tinctures, infusions, and poultices, offer various ways to extract and use the beneficial compounds present in herbs. In this chapter, we will explore these preparation techniques to create effective herbal remedies.

1. Herbal Teas: Herbal teas, also known as herbal infusions or tisanes, are one of the simplest and most common ways to use medicinal plants. To prepare an herbal tea:

● Boil water and pour it over the desired amount of dried or fresh herbs in a teapot or cup.

● Cover the container and let the herbs steep for the recommended time (usually 5-15 minutes, depending on the herb).

● Strain the liquid to remove the plant material, and your herbal tea is ready to drink.

Herbal teas are suitable for various purposes, such as calming nerves, aiding digestion, promoting sleep, or soothing sore throats.

1. Tinctures: Tinctures are concentrated liquid extracts made by soaking herbs in alcohol or a mixture of alcohol and water. The alcohol acts as a solvent, extracting the active compounds from the plant material. To make a tincture:

● Fill a glass jar with the chosen dried herb or herb mixture.

● Cover the herbs with alcohol (vodka, rum, or brandy) to fully submerge them.

● Seal the jar tightly and store it in a cool, dark place for several weeks, shaking it daily to enhance extraction.

● After the steeping period, strain the liquid through a fine mesh or cheesecloth, and transfer it to amber glass dropper bottles for storage.

Tinctures offer a long shelf life and provide a convenient way to administer precise doses of herbal remedies.

1. Herbal Infusions: Herbal infusions are similar to teas but involve longer steeping times to extract more of the plant's constituents. Infusions are typically used for extracting the medicinal properties of roots, barks, and tougher plant parts. To make an herbal infusion:

● Boil water and pour it over the desired amount of dried or fresh herbs in a heat proof container.

● Cover the container and let the herbs steep for a more extended period, often around 30 minutes to several hours.

● Strain the liquid to remove the plant material.

Herbal infusions can be consumed as a medicinal drink or used externally as a wash or compress.

1. Herbal Poultices: Herbal poultices involve applying fresh or dried herbs directly to the skin to address various skin conditions or localized issues. To create a herbal poultice:

● Grind or crush the selected fresh or dried herbs to create a paste.

● Apply the herbal paste directly to the affected area.

● Cover the poultice with a clean cloth or bandage to hold it in place.

Herbal poultices can be beneficial for soothing skin irritations, reducing inflammation, and promoting healing.

Chapter 3: The Top Medicinal Plants and Their Uses

1.Aloe Vera: Soothing Skin Ailments, Aiding Digestion, and Promoting Wound Healing

Aloe Vera, also known as the "plant of immortality," is a well-known and widely used medicinal plant with a history of healing properties dating back thousands of years. Native to the Arabian Peninsula, Aloe Vera is now cultivated in various regions worldwide due to its exceptional therapeutic benefits. In this chapter, we will explore how Aloe Vera can be used to soothe skin ailments, aid digestion, and promote wound healing.

1. Soothing Skin Ailments: Aloe Vera's gel-like substance found in the leaves contains a rich combination of vitamins, minerals, amino acids, enzymes, and polysaccharides that contribute to its skin-soothing properties. When applied topically, Aloe Vera gel can provide relief for various skin conditions, including:

● Sunburn: Aloe Vera's cooling effect helps alleviate the discomfort and redness associated with sunburn. It can also support skin healing and minimize peeling.

● Irritated Skin: Aloe Vera can be used to soothe and reduce inflammation caused by minor skin irritations, insect bites, or allergic reactions.

● Dry Skin: Aloe Vera's moisturizing properties help hydrate and nourish dry skin, promoting a smoother and more supple complexion.

1. Aiding Digestion: Aloe Vera has been traditionally used to

support digestive health. The plant contains compounds like aloin and aloesin, known for their potential laxative effects. However, it is essential to exercise caution with internal use, as Aloe Vera can be potent and may cause gastrointestinal discomfort if consumed in excessive amounts. To use Aloe Vera for digestive support:

• Aloe Vera Juice: Commercially prepared Aloe Vera juice, when consumed in moderate amounts, may help alleviate occasional constipation and promote regular bowel movements.

• Note: Always follow the recommended dosage guidelines and consult a healthcare professional before using Aloe Vera internally, especially if you have any gastrointestinal issues or are taking medications.

1. Promoting Wound Healing: Aloe Vera's wound-healing properties are well-established, making it a valuable natural remedy for minor cuts, burns, and abrasions. The plant's gel contains compounds that:

• Stimulate Cell Growth: Aloe Vera gel contains growth hormones that aid in the production of new skin cells, accelerating the wound healing process.

• Anti-Inflammatory: The anti-inflammatory properties of Aloe Vera help reduce redness, swelling, and discomfort around wounds.

• Antimicrobial: Aloe Vera's natural antimicrobial properties protect wounds from infection, helping to maintain a sterile environment.

To use Aloe Vera for wound healing, gently apply the fresh gel extracted from the leaf directly onto the affected area. Alternatively, commercially available Aloe Vera gel or ointments can be used for this purpose.

2.Ginger: Easing Nausea, Reducing Inflammation, and Supporting Digestion

Ginger, scientifically known as Zingiber officinale, is a well-regarded medicinal plant that has been used for centuries in various traditional healing practices. Native to Southeast Asia, ginger is now cultivated worldwide for its numerous health benefits and culinary uses. In this chapter, we will explore how ginger can be used to ease nausea, reduce inflammation, and support digestion.

1. Easing Nausea: Ginger is widely recognized for its effectiveness in alleviating nausea and vomiting, making it a valuable remedy for various conditions, including:

● Morning Sickness: Pregnant women often use ginger to help relieve morning sickness and nausea during pregnancy. It is considered safe when used in moderation, but pregnant individuals should consult their healthcare provider before using ginger or any other herbal remedy.

● Motion Sickness: Ginger can be beneficial in reducing motion sickness symptoms, such as dizziness and nausea, when traveling by car, boat, or airplane.

● Chemotherapy-Induced Nausea: Some studies suggest that ginger may help reduce nausea and vomiting associated with chemotherapy treatment, but it is essential to discuss its use with a healthcare professional.

To use ginger for easing nausea, you can consume it as fresh ginger slices, ginger tea, ginger candies, or in powdered form. Start with small amounts and gradually increase as needed.

1. Reducing Inflammation: Ginger contains bioactive compounds like gingerol and shogaol, which possess potent anti-inflammatory properties. These compounds help to reduce inflammation in the body and may be beneficial for conditions such as:

● Osteoarthritis: Studies have shown that regular consumption of ginger may help alleviate symptoms of osteoarthritis, including joint pain and stiffness.

● Muscle Pain: Ginger's anti-inflammatory properties can aid in reducing muscle pain and soreness after intense exercise or physical activity.

● Inflammatory Bowel Diseases: Some research suggests that ginger may have a beneficial effect on reducing inflammation in conditions like ulcerative colitis and Crohn's disease.

Incorporate ginger into your diet regularly by adding it to meals, using it in cooking, or consuming ginger supplements, but always consult a healthcare professional before using ginger supplements, especially if you are taking blood-thinning medications or have a bleeding disorder.

1. Supporting Digestion: Ginger is renowned for its ability to support digestive health by promoting proper digestion and relieving gastrointestinal discomfort. It aids in various digestive issues, such as:

● Indigestion: Ginger can help ease indigestion by promoting the movement of food through the digestive tract and reducing bloating and gas.

● Nausea and Upset Stomach: As mentioned earlier, ginger's anti-nausea properties can be beneficial for soothing upset stomachs and improving overall digestion.

● Irritable Bowel Syndrome (IBS): Some individuals with IBS find relief from symptoms like abdominal pain and bloating by incorporating ginger into their diet.

To support digestion, you can consume ginger as fresh ginger tea, ginger-infused water, or include it in cooking to enhance the flavor of various dishes.

3.Echinacea: Strengthening the Immune System and Fighting Respiratory Infections

Echinacea, commonly known as the purple coneflower, is a flowering plant native to North America. It has a long history of use in traditional Native American medicine as a potent immune-boosting herb. Today, echinacea is widely recognized for its ability to strengthen the immune system and help combat respiratory infections. In this chapter, we will explore how echinacea can be used to enhance immune function and support respiratory health.

1. Strengthening the Immune System: Echinacea is celebrated for its immunomodulatory properties, meaning it can help regulate and enhance the body's immune response. The plant's roots, flowers, and leaves contain active compounds such as polysaccharides, alkamides, and flavonoids, which play a role in supporting immune function. Echinacea is believed to:

● Activate Immune Cells: Echinacea can stimulate the activity of immune cells, such as macrophages and white blood cells, enhancing their ability to detect and combat infections.

● Increase Antibody Production: The herb may stimulate the production of antibodies, proteins that target and neutralize foreign invaders, thus bolstering the body's defense mechanisms.

● Enhance Natural Killer (NK) Cell Activity: Echinacea may increase the activity of NK cells, which play a crucial role in identifying and eliminating infected or abnormal cells.

To support immune health, echinacea supplements, teas, or tinctures are commonly used. Regular and consistent use during times of increased susceptibility to illnesses may offer immune-boosting benefits.

1. Fighting Respiratory Infections: Echinacea's immune-enhancing properties also make it a valuable ally in combating respiratory infections, particularly those caused by viruses and bacteria. It is often employed to:

● Reduce the Severity of Colds and Flu: Echinacea may help reduce the severity and duration of symptoms associated with the common cold and flu, such as cough, sore throat, and nasal congestion.

● Support Upper Respiratory Health: The herb can assist in maintaining the health of the upper respiratory tract, making it useful in managing conditions like bronchitis and sinusitis.

● Enhance Recovery: When taken at the first signs of respiratory infection, echinacea may aid in a quicker recovery by supporting the body's natural defense mechanisms.

When using echinacea to fight respiratory infections, it is essential to start using it at the earliest onset of symptoms for maximum effectiveness.

1. Precautions and Considerations: While echinacea is generally considered safe for most people, some individuals may experience mild side effects such as an upset stomach or allergic reactions. As with any herbal remedy, it is crucial to:

● Consult a Healthcare Professional: Before using echinacea, especially if you have underlying health conditions, are pregnant or breastfeeding, or are taking medications, it's essential to consult a qualified healthcare professional.

● Use with Caution: Echinacea is not recommended for those with autoimmune disorders, as it may stimulate the immune system and potentially exacerbate the condition.

4.Chamomile: Calming Anxiety, Promoting Sleep, and Soothing Digestive Discomfort

Chamomile, a gentle and aromatic herb, has been cherished for centuries for its calming and healing properties. There are two main types of chamomile commonly used for medicinal purposes: German chamomile (Matricaria chamomilla) and Roman chamomile (Chamaemelum nobile). Both varieties share similar therapeutic benefits, and they have a long history of traditional use. In this chapter, we will explore how chamomile can be used to calm anxiety, promote sleep, and soothe digestive discomfort.

1. Calming Anxiety: Chamomile is well-known for its anxiolytic effects, which help reduce feelings of anxiety and promote relaxation. The plant contains compounds like apigenin, bisabolol, and flavonoids that contribute to its calming properties. Chamomile can be used to:

● Reduce General Anxiety: Drinking chamomile tea or using chamomile essential oil in aromatherapy may help alleviate feelings of restlessness and promote a sense of calmness.

● Relieve Nervous Tension: In times of stress or tension, chamomile can be consumed as a tea to help ease nervousness and promote relaxation.

Chamomile's gentle nature makes it a safe choice for individuals seeking natural remedies for anxiety, but it is essential to remember that severe or chronic anxiety may require professional help.

1. Promoting Sleep: Chamomile's calming effects extend to its potential to support restful sleep. Drinking chamomile tea before bedtime can:

- Improve Sleep Quality: Chamomile may help individuals fall asleep faster and experience deeper, more restorative sleep.

- Reduce Insomnia: People experiencing mild insomnia may find relief with chamomile, as it may help regulate sleep patterns.

Enjoy a warm cup of chamomile tea about an hour before bedtime to help relax the mind and body for a peaceful night's sleep.

1. Soothing Digestive Discomfort: Chamomile has been used for centuries to ease digestive discomfort and support gastrointestinal health. It can be beneficial for various digestive issues, including:

- Indigestion: Drinking chamomile tea after meals may help alleviate bloating, gas, and indigestion.

- Upset Stomach: Chamomile's anti-inflammatory properties can help soothe an upset stomach and reduce irritation.

- Colic and Infant Discomfort: Chamomile tea is sometimes used to ease colic and digestive discomfort in infants, but always consult a pediatrician before introducing chamomile to a baby's diet.

Chamomile's mild and soothing nature makes it a popular choice for those with sensitive stomachs or mild gastrointestinal discomfort.

5.Turmeric: Anti-Inflammatory Properties, Aiding Digestion, and Supporting Joint Health

Turmeric, scientifically known as Curcuma longa, is a vibrant yellow-orange spice that belongs to the ginger family. Originating from South Asia, turmeric has been used for centuries in traditional medicine and culinary practices. Its active compound, curcumin, is responsible for its impressive health benefits. In this chapter, we will explore how turmeric can be used for its anti-inflammatory properties, aiding digestion, and supporting joint health.

1. Anti-Inflammatory Properties: One of the most well-known and researched properties of turmeric is its potent anti-inflammatory effect. Curcumin, the primary bioactive compound in turmeric, acts as a powerful antioxidant and modulates various inflammatory pathways in the body. Turmeric can be used to:

● Reduce Inflammation: Curcumin helps combat chronic inflammation, which is associated with various chronic diseases, including arthritis, heart disease, and certain cancers.

● Alleviate Joint Pain: Turmeric's anti-inflammatory properties may provide relief for individuals with joint pain and stiffness caused by inflammatory conditions such as rheumatoid arthritis and osteoarthritis.

Incorporating turmeric into your diet regularly can contribute to overall inflammation reduction and support better health.

1. Aiding Digestion: Turmeric has a long history of use in traditional medicine to support digestive health. It aids digestion in several ways:

● Stimulating Bile Production: Turmeric stimulates the production of bile by the gallbladder, which aids in the breakdown of fats and supports better digestion.

● Relieving Indigestion: The anti-inflammatory properties of turmeric can help ease indigestion, bloating, and gas.

● Supporting Liver Health: Turmeric may benefit liver health by promoting detoxification and protecting the liver from oxidative stress.

You can incorporate turmeric into your diet by using it as a spice in cooking, adding it to smoothies, or taking turmeric supplements in consultation with a healthcare professional.

1. Supporting Joint Health: As mentioned earlier, turmeric's anti-inflammatory effects can have a positive impact on joint health. It is often used to:

● Improve Mobility: Turmeric may help improve joint flexibility and ease joint discomfort, enhancing overall joint function.

● Manage Arthritis Symptoms: People with arthritis may find relief from joint pain and inflammation by including turmeric in their daily routine.

Regular use of turmeric, along with a balanced diet and lifestyle, may support joint health and reduce discomfort associated with joint conditions.

6.Peppermint: Relieving Headaches, Easing Indigestion, and Alleviating Respiratory Issues

Peppermint (Mentha × piperita) is a well-known and aromatic herb that has been used for centuries for its numerous health benefits and refreshing flavor. A hybrid of spearmint and watermint, peppermint is native to Europe but is now widely cultivated around the world. In this chapter, we will explore how peppermint can be used to relieve headaches, ease indigestion, and alleviate respiratory issues.

1. Relieving Headaches: Peppermint has been recognized for its ability to alleviate headaches and migraines. The menthol present in peppermint acts as a muscle relaxant and a mild analgesic, offering relief from tension headaches and migraines. Peppermint can be used to:

● Relieve Tension Headaches: Applying diluted peppermint essential oil topically to the temples and forehead can help ease muscle tension and reduce headache discomfort.

● Ease Migraines: Inhaling peppermint essential oil or using peppermint-infused balms may provide relief from migraine symptoms and reduce sensitivity to light and sound.

It is essential to dilute peppermint essential oil with a carrier oil before applying it to the skin to avoid skin irritation.

1. Easing Indigestion: Peppermint is widely recognized for its beneficial effects on digestion and can help ease various digestive issues, including:

- Relieve Indigestion: Drinking peppermint tea after meals can aid digestion and alleviate symptoms of indigestion, such as bloating and gas.

- Reduce Abdominal Pain: Peppermint's muscle relaxant properties can help soothe abdominal muscles and reduce cramping.

Peppermint tea is a gentle and soothing remedy for digestive discomfort, and its pleasant taste makes it an enjoyable after-dinner drink.

1. Alleviating Respiratory Issues: Peppermint's menthol content contributes to its ability to alleviate respiratory issues and improve breathing. Peppermint can be used to:

- Clear Sinuses: Inhaling peppermint essential oil or using a steam inhalation with peppermint leaves can help open up congested sinuses and improve airflow.

- Soothe Throat Irritation: Drinking warm peppermint tea with honey can help soothe a sore throat and reduce coughing.

Peppermint's invigorating aroma also contributes to a sense of freshness and relief during respiratory discomfort.

7.Lavender: Reducing Stress and Anxiety, Promoting Relaxation, and Aiding Sleep

Lavender (Lavandula angustifolia) is a fragrant herb known for its calming and therapeutic properties. Native to the Mediterranean region, lavender is now cultivated globally for its versatile uses in both traditional and modern medicine. In this chapter, we will explore how lavender can be used to reduce stress and anxiety, promote relaxation, and aid in achieving restful sleep.

1. Reducing Stress and Anxiety: Lavender is renowned for its anxiolytic effects, making it a popular remedy for reducing stress and anxiety. The soothing aroma of lavender essential oil can have a calming effect on the nervous system and promote relaxation. Lavender can be used to:

● Relieve Stress: Inhaling lavender essential oil or using lavender-infused products can help alleviate feelings of stress and tension.

● Calm Nervousness: Lavender's calming properties may help ease nervousness and promote a sense of tranquility during anxious moments.

Inhaling lavender essential oil through a diffuser or using lavender-based aromatherapy products can be beneficial for relaxation.

1. Promoting Relaxation: The pleasant and soothing scent of lavender makes it an excellent choice for promoting relaxation and unwinding after a long day. Lavender can be used to:

- Create a Relaxing Environment: Adding a few drops of lavender essential oil to a bath or using it in room sprays can create a calming atmosphere.

- Ease Muscle Tension: Applying diluted lavender essential oil topically to tense muscles can help relax and soothe them.

Taking time to enjoy lavender-infused activities, such as a warm bath with lavender oil or using lavender-scented body lotions, can enhance relaxation.

1. Aiding Sleep: Lavender's calming properties extend to its potential to improve sleep quality and promote restful slumber. Lavender can be used to:

- Enhance Sleep: Inhaling lavender's aroma before bedtime or using lavender essential oil in a diffuser can help improve sleep quality and reduce sleep disturbances.

- Combat Insomnia: Lavender may be beneficial for individuals experiencing mild insomnia, as it can help relax the mind and body, facilitating sleep.

Using lavender-based products, such as lavender-infused sleep masks or linen sprays, can create a sleep-conducive environment

8.Garlic: Boosting the Immune System, Supporting Heart Health, and Fighting Infections

Garlic (Allium sativum) is a pungent and flavorful herb widely recognized for its numerous health benefits and culinary uses. Native to Central Asia, garlic has been used for centuries in traditional medicine for its medicinal properties. In this chapter, we will explore how garlic can be used to boost the immune system, support heart health, and fight infections.

1. Boosting the Immune System: Garlic is celebrated for its immunomodulatory effects, meaning it can enhance the body's immune response and help defend against infections. Garlic contains compounds like allicin, which contribute to its immune-boosting properties. Garlic can be used to:

● Strengthen the Immune Response: Regular consumption of garlic may help improve the activity of immune cells, such as white blood cells, increasing the body's ability to fight off infections.

● Reduce the Severity of Illness: Garlic's immune-enhancing effects may help reduce the severity and duration of common illnesses like the cold and flu.

To benefit from garlic's immune-boosting properties, incorporate fresh or cooked garlic into your meals regularly.

1. Supporting Heart Health: Garlic has long been associated with heart health, and scientific research supports its positive impact on cardiovascular well-being. Garlic can be used to:

● Lower Blood Pressure: Garlic has been shown to have a modest effect in reducing blood pressure, which may be beneficial for individuals with hypertension.

● Improve Cholesterol Levels: Regular consumption of garlic may help reduce total cholesterol and LDL cholesterol levels, supporting heart health.

● Enhance Blood Circulation: Garlic's ability to improve blood flow and vasodilation may contribute to overall cardiovascular health.

Adding garlic to your diet, either raw or cooked, may provide cardiovascular benefits and support heart health.

1. Fighting Infections: Garlic is renowned for its antimicrobial properties, making it a valuable ally in fighting infections caused by bacteria, viruses, and fungi. Garlic can be used to:

● Combat Common Infections: Garlic's antimicrobial effects may help in treating and preventing various infections, such as colds, flu, and even some types of food poisoning.

● Support Wound Healing: Garlic's antimicrobial properties can aid in preventing infection and promoting healing when applied topically to minor wounds.

Garlic's natural antimicrobial properties make it a useful addition to your natural medicine cabinet.

9.Ginkgo Biloba: Enhancing Memory and Cognitive Function, Supporting Brain Health

Ginkgo biloba, commonly known as ginkgo, is one of the oldest living tree species on Earth and has a rich history of use in traditional Chinese medicine. The leaves of the ginkgo tree are prized for their potential cognitive benefits and medicinal properties. In this chapter, we will explore how ginkgo biloba can be used to enhance memory and cognitive function, as well as support brain health.

1. Enhancing Memory and Cognitive Function: Ginkgo biloba is widely regarded for its potential to enhance memory and cognitive abilities, particularly in aging individuals. The primary bioactive compounds in ginkgo leaves, including flavonoids and terpenoids, have antioxidant and neuroprotective properties. Ginkgo biloba can be used to:

● Improve Memory: Regular consumption of ginkgo biloba may aid in improving memory, especially in older adults experiencing mild cognitive decline.

● Enhance Cognitive Function: Ginkgo may support various cognitive functions, such as attention, focus, and information processing speed.

To potentially benefit from ginkgo biloba's memory-enhancing properties, it is often taken as a supplement in the form of capsules or tablets. As with any supplement, it is essential to consult a qualified healthcare professional for personalized guidance and appropriate dosages.

1. Supporting Brain Health: Ginkgo biloba is believed to support overall brain health and function through various mechanisms,

including:

• Antioxidant Effects: Ginkgo's antioxidant properties help protect brain cells from oxidative stress, which is associated with brain aging and cognitive decline.

• Increasing Blood Flow: Ginkgo has been shown to enhance blood flow to the brain, which may promote better oxygen and nutrient delivery to brain cells.

• Neuroprotection: Ginkgo's neuroprotective effects may help shield brain cells from damage and support their survival.

While research on ginkgo's benefits is ongoing, it is thought that the herb's brain-boosting properties may offer long-term advantages for overall brain health.

.

10.Calendula: Soothing Skin Irritations, Promoting Wound Healing, and Reducing Inflammation

Calendula, also known as marigold (Calendula officinalis), is a vibrant and cheerful herb with a long history of medicinal use. Native to Mediterranean regions, calendula is now cultivated worldwide for its soothing and healing properties. In this chapter, we will explore how calendula can be used to soothe skin irritations, promote wound healing, and reduce inflammation.

1. Soothing Skin Irritations: Calendula's anti-inflammatory and emollient properties make it an excellent remedy for soothing various skin irritations. Calendula can be used to:

• Relieve Minor Burns: Calendula ointments or creams can provide relief for minor burns and help reduce redness and discomfort.

• Soothe Eczema and Dermatitis: Calendula-infused oils or creams can help ease the itching and inflammation associated with eczema and dermatitis.

• Reduce Skin Redness: Applying calendula topically can help reduce skin redness caused by irritation, rashes, or allergies.

Calendula is gentle on the skin, making it suitable for use on sensitive and delicate skin areas.

1. Promoting Wound Healing: Calendula's wound-healing properties have made it a popular choice for assisting in the recovery of minor wounds and cuts. Calendula can be used to:

• Accelerate Wound Healing: Applying calendula ointments or creams to minor wounds can help stimulate the formation of new tissue and speed up the healing process.

• Reduce Scarring: Regular use of calendula on healing wounds may help minimize scarring and support better skin regeneration.

Calendula's ability to promote wound healing makes it a valuable addition to natural first aid kits.

1. Reducing Inflammation: Calendula's anti-inflammatory effects can be beneficial for reducing inflammation on the skin's surface. Calendula can be used to:

• Ease Skin Inflammation: Topical application of calendula can help soothe skin inflammation caused by minor skin irritations, insect bites, or sunburn.

• Calm Irritated Skin: Calendula's gentle nature can help calm and soothe irritated skin, making it suitable for various skin types.

Using calendula-infused oils or creams on inflamed skin can provide relief and support the skin's natural healing process.

Chapter 4: Herbal Remedies for Common Ailments

Section 1: Herbal Treatments for Coughs, Colds, and Flu Symptoms

Coughs, colds, and flu are common respiratory illnesses that can cause discomfort and disrupt daily life. Herbal remedies offer natural and time-tested options for managing these ailments and alleviating symptoms. In this section, we will explore several herbal treatments known for their effectiveness in providing relief from coughs, colds, and flu symptoms.

1. Echinacea (Echinacea purpurea): Echinacea, with its immune-boosting properties, can be beneficial for preventing and managing colds and flu. It can help stimulate the immune system and reduce the severity and duration of symptoms. Echinacea supplements or herbal teas made from echinacea flowers and roots can be taken at the first signs of illness to support the body's defense against viral infections.

2. Elderberry (Sambucus nigra): Elderberry has been used for centuries as a remedy for respiratory infections, including colds and flu. Elderberries are rich in antioxidants and vitamin C, which can help bolster the immune system and reduce inflammation. Elderberry syrup or elderberry-infused teas are popular choices for soothing sore throats and supporting the body's recovery from viral infections.

3. Ginger (Zingiber officinale): Ginger's warming and anti-inflammatory properties make it an excellent herbal remedy for cold and flu symptoms. Ginger tea, prepared from fresh ginger root or ginger tea bags, can help relieve sore throats, ease congestion, and reduce nausea and vomiting associated with

the flu.

4. Peppermint (Mentha × piperita): Peppermint is well-regarded for its decongestant and soothing properties. Peppermint tea or peppermint essential oil inhalations can help clear nasal passages, reduce coughing, and alleviate headaches associated with colds and flu.

5. Thyme (Thymus vulgaris): Thyme is an herb with antimicrobial properties, making it beneficial for respiratory infections. Thyme tea or thyme-infused steam inhalations can help soothe coughs and reduce inflammation in the respiratory tract.

6. Licorice Root (Glycyrrhiza glabra): Licorice root has expectorant and anti-inflammatory properties, making it useful for relieving coughs and soothing sore throats. Licorice root tea or lozenges can help ease coughing and provide relief from irritation in the throat.

7. Marshmallow Root (Althaea officinalis): Marshmallow root is known for its mucilage content, which can help soothe irritated throat and respiratory tissues. Marshmallow root tea or lozenges can provide relief from coughs and ease throat discomfort.

It's important to remember that while herbal remedies can be effective for managing mild coughs, colds, and flu symptoms, they are not substitutes for medical treatment, especially in severe cases. If symptoms persist or worsen, or if you have underlying health conditions, it is essential to seek advice from a qualified healthcare professional.

Section 2: Managing Digestive Issues and Promoting Gut Health with Herbal Remedies

Digestive issues such as indigestion, bloating, gas, and occasional constipation can cause discomfort and disrupt daily life. Herbal remedies offer natural and gentle ways to manage digestive problems and promote gut health. In this section, we will explore several herbal treatments known for their effectiveness in supporting digestion and maintaining a healthy gut.

1. Peppermint (Mentha × piperita): Peppermint is a versatile herb that can help soothe various digestive issues. Peppermint tea or peppermint oil capsules can be used to:

● Relieve Indigestion: Peppermint's carminative properties can ease indigestion, bloating, and gas.

● Reduce Irritable Bowel Syndrome (IBS) Symptoms: Peppermint may alleviate abdominal pain and discomfort associated with IBS.

1. Ginger (Zingiber officinale): Ginger is renowned for its digestive benefits and can be used to:

● Improve Digestion: Ginger tea or fresh ginger root can stimulate digestion and help relieve indigestion.

● Reduce Nausea: Ginger can ease nausea and vomiting, making it particularly helpful for morning sickness and motion sickness.

1. Chamomile (Matricaria chamomilla): Chamomile's calming properties extend to the digestive system and can be used to:

• Soothe Indigestion: Chamomile tea can help ease indigestion and promote relaxation after meals.

• Relieve Upset Stomach: Chamomile's anti-inflammatory properties can help soothe an upset stomach.

1.   Fennel (Foeniculum vulgare): Fennel seeds can be used to:

• Ease Bloating and Gas: Fennel seeds can be chewed or brewed into tea to alleviate bloating and gas.

• Support Digestive Health: Fennel's carminative properties make it useful for maintaining digestive health.

1.   Licorice Root (Glycyrrhiza glabra): Licorice root can help with various digestive issues, including:

• Relieve Heartburn: Licorice root can help soothe heartburn and acid reflux.

• Support Gastric Lining: Licorice root can help protect and support the gastric lining.

1.   Dandelion Root (Taraxacum officinale): Dandelion root tea can support digestive health by:

• Aiding Digestion: Dandelion root can stimulate digestive juices and support healthy digestion.

• Acting as a Gentle Laxative: Dandelion root can help with occasional constipation.

It's important to remember that individual responses to herbal remedies can vary, and some herbs may interact with medications or have contraindications for certain health conditions. Always consult a qualified healthcare professional before using herbal remedies, especially if you are pregnant, breastfeeding, or have underlying health issues.

Section 3: Natural Solutions for Stress, Anxiety, and Sleep Disturbances

Stress, anxiety, and sleep disturbances can significantly impact our well-being and quality of life. Herbal remedies offer natural and soothing alternatives for managing these emotional and sleep-related challenges. In this section, we will explore several herbal treatments known for their effectiveness in reducing stress, alleviating anxiety, and promoting restful sleep.

1. Lavender (Lavandula angustifolia): Lavender is renowned for its calming properties and can be used to:

● Reduce Stress and Anxiety: Lavender essential oil or lavender-infused products can help promote relaxation and ease feelings of stress and anxiety.

● Aid Sleep: Inhaling lavender's aroma before bedtime or using lavender-infused products can support restful sleep and improve sleep quality.

1. Chamomile (Matricaria chamomilla): Chamomile is a gentle herb that can help ease stress, anxiety, and sleep disturbances by:

● Calming Anxiety: Chamomile tea or chamomile-infused aromatherapy can help reduce feelings of restlessness and promote relaxation.

● Promoting Sleep: Chamomile's soothing effects can aid in falling asleep faster and achieving deeper sleep.

1. Valerian (Valeriana officinalis): Valerian root is a sedative herb

that can help with anxiety and sleep issues by:

● Reducing Anxiety: Valerian can help ease nervousness and promote a sense of calmness.

● Improving Sleep Quality: Valerian root supplements can support better sleep and reduce insomnia symptoms.

1. Passionflower (Passiflora incarnata): Passionflower is a calming herb that can be used to:

● Relieve Anxiety: Passionflower can help alleviate anxiety symptoms and promote relaxation.

● Enhance Sleep: Passionflower's sedative properties may improve sleep quality and aid in falling asleep.

1. Lemon Balm (Melissa officinalis): Lemon balm is a soothing herb that can help with stress, anxiety, and sleep disturbances by:

● Calming Nervousness: Lemon balm tea or aromatherapy can help ease nervousness and promote relaxation.

● Supporting Sleep: Lemon balm's calming effects can improve sleep quality and reduce sleep disturbances.

1. Ashwagandha (Withania somnifera): Ashwagandha is an adaptogenic herb that can help the body adapt to stress and:

● Reduce Stress and Anxiety: Ashwagandha supplements can help regulate the body's stress response and reduce anxiety symptoms.

- Support Sleep: Ashwagandha's calming effects may contribute to better sleep quality and improved overall sleep patterns.

As with any herbal remedy, individual responses may vary, and it is essential to consult a qualified healthcare professional before using herbal treatments, especially if you are pregnant, breastfeeding, or taking medications.

Section 4: Herbal First Aid for Minor Injuries and Skin Conditions

Herbal remedies can be valuable additions to your first aid kit, offering natural and soothing alternatives for managing minor injuries and skin conditions. In this section, we will explore several herbal treatments known for their effectiveness in providing first aid for cuts, scrapes, burns, and various skin issues.

1. Aloe Vera (Aloe barbadensis miller): Aloe vera is a versatile plant that can help with various skin issues and minor injuries by:

● Soothing Burns: Aloe vera gel can provide relief and aid in the healing of minor burns and sunburns.

● Promoting Wound Healing: Aloe vera can be applied topically to cuts and scrapes to promote faster healing and reduce inflammation.

1. Calendula (Calendula officinalis): Calendula is a gentle herb that can be used for minor injuries and skin conditions by:

● Healing Wounds: Calendula ointments or creams can help heal cuts, scrapes, and minor skin irritations.

● Soothing Skin Inflammation: Calendula's anti-inflammatory properties can help reduce redness and irritation on the skin.

1. Comfrey (Symphytum officinale): Comfrey has been traditionally used to aid in the healing of bruises, sprains, and minor fractures by:

• Reducing Swelling: Comfrey poultices or creams can help reduce swelling and inflammation associated with minor injuries.

• Promoting Tissue Repair: Comfrey can support the regeneration of damaged tissues and promote faster healing.

1. Tea Tree Oil (Melaleuca alternifolia): Tea tree oil has natural antimicrobial properties and can be used for various skin issues by:

• Treating Cuts and Scrapes: Diluted tea tree oil can be applied to minor cuts and scrapes to prevent infection and aid in healing.

• Addressing Skin Infections: Tea tree oil can help with fungal and bacterial skin infections, such as athlete's foot or acne.

1. Witch Hazel (Hamamelis virginiana): Witch hazel is a natural astringent that can be used to:

• Cleanse Wounds: Witch hazel can be applied to clean cuts and scrapes to help keep the area free from bacteria.

• Relieve Skin Irritations: Witch hazel can soothe skin conditions like insect bites and rashes.

It's important to note that while herbal remedies can be effective for minor injuries and skin conditions, they are not substitutes for professional medical care in severe cases. Always consult a qualified healthcare professional for serious injuries or persistent skin issues.

Chapter 5: Safety and Precautions

● Understanding Potential Side Effects and Interactions with Medications

While herbal remedies can offer natural and beneficial solutions for various health concerns, it is essential to approach their use with caution and awareness of potential side effects and interactions, especially when combining them with medications. In this chapter, we will explore the importance of safety and precautions when using herbal remedies.

1. Consult a Healthcare Professional: Before starting any herbal treatment, it is crucial to consult a qualified healthcare professional, such as a doctor, naturopath, or herbalist. They can provide personalized guidance based on your medical history, current health conditions, and medications. This is especially important if you are pregnant, breastfeeding, or have underlying health issues.

2. Identify Allergies and Sensitivities: Individuals may have allergies or sensitivities to certain herbs. Before using a new herbal remedy, perform a patch test on a small area of the skin to check for allergic reactions. Discontinue use immediately if any adverse reactions occur.

3. Potential Side Effects: Herbs, like conventional medications, may have side effects. Common side effects of certain herbs may include digestive upset, skin reactions, drowsiness, or headaches. Monitor your body's response to herbal remedies and discontinue use if side effects are experienced.

4. Interactions with Medications: Herbs can interact with prescription medications, over-the-counter drugs, and other supplements, potentially affecting their efficacy or causing adverse reactions. Some herbs may increase or decrease the

effects of certain medications, leading to unintended consequences. Always inform your healthcare professional about all the herbs and supplements you are taking to avoid harmful interactions.

5. Dosage and Duration: Follow recommended dosages and guidelines for herbal remedies. Avoid taking excessive amounts of herbs, as this can lead to toxicity or other complications. Do not use herbal remedies for an extended period without consulting a healthcare professional.

6. Quality and Source of Herbs: Ensure you are using high-quality herbs from reputable sources. Contaminated or adulterated herbs can pose health risks.

7. Pregnancy and Breastfeeding: Certain herbs are contraindicated during pregnancy and breastfeeding. Always consult a healthcare professional before using any herbal remedy during these stages of life.

8. Children and Elderly: Some herbs may not be suitable for children or the elderly. Seek professional advice before using herbal remedies for these age groups.

9. Chronic Health Conditions: If you have chronic health conditions like diabetes, hypertension, or autoimmune disorders, exercise extra caution when using herbal remedies. Some herbs may interact with medications used to manage these conditions.

○ **Identifying Poisonous Plants and Avoiding Accidental Ingestion**

In the natural world, there are both beneficial and harmful plants, including poisonous ones that can pose serious health risks if ingested. Identifying poisonous plants and understanding how to avoid accidental ingestion is essential for ensuring your safety and the safety of those around you. In this chapter, we will explore tips for identifying poisonous plants and adopting practices to avoid accidental ingestion.

1. Educate Yourself: Familiarize yourself with common poisonous plants in your region. Obtain reliable field guides, consult local plant experts, or attend workshops on plant identification. Learn to recognize distinctive characteristics, such as color, shape, and leaf arrangements, to distinguish poisonous plants from harmless ones.

2. Avoid Contact: Exercise caution when exploring unfamiliar outdoor areas, especially if you are not confident in plant identification. Avoid touching or ingesting any plant that you are uncertain about, as contact alone can sometimes cause skin irritation or allergic reactions.

3. Teach Children: Educate children about the importance of not eating or touching plants without adult supervision. Teach them to identify harmful plants in their surroundings and to seek help from an adult if they encounter an unfamiliar plant.

4. Stay on Designated Trails: When hiking or exploring natural areas, stick to designated trails and pathways. Avoid wandering into dense vegetation or areas where you may encounter unfamiliar plants.

5. Use Protective Gear: Wear gloves and protective clothing, especially when gardening or handling plants with potential toxins. This can help prevent accidental contact and ingestion.

6. Know Poison Ivy, Oak, and Sumac: Learn to identify and avoid common poisonous plants like poison ivy, poison oak, and poison sumac. These plants can cause severe skin irritation upon contact.

7. Avoid Using Unidentified Plants: Avoid using plants from the wild or your garden in cooking, teas, or homemade remedies unless you are confident in their identification and safety.

8. Keep Plants Away from Pets: Ensure that your pets cannot access or ingest poisonous plants. Some common houseplants, such as certain varieties of lilies and philodendrons, can be toxic to pets.

9. Contact Poison Control: In case of accidental ingestion or contact with a potentially poisonous plant, contact your local poison control center or seek medical attention immediately.

● Best practices for consulting healthcare professionals and herbalists when necessary

Consulting healthcare professionals and herbalists when necessary is essential for making informed decisions about your health and well-being. Here are some best practices to ensure you have a productive and beneficial consultation:

1. Be Prepared: Before the consultation, make a list of your current health concerns, symptoms, and any medications or supplements you are taking. Gather relevant medical records and information about your medical history.

2. Choose Qualified Professionals: Seek out licensed healthcare professionals, such as medical doctors, naturopathic doctors, or registered herbalists. Look for individuals with proper education, certification, and experience in their respective fields.

3. Research Credentials: Verify the credentials and qualifications

of the healthcare professionals or herbalists you plan to consult. Check for any specialized training in herbal medicine or relevant experience.

4. Communicate Clearly: During the consultation, be open and honest about your health concerns, lifestyle, and any previous experiences with herbal remedies. Provide accurate and detailed information to help the professional understand your unique situation better.

5. Share Medications and Supplements: Inform the healthcare professional or herbalist about all medications, supplements, and herbal remedies you are currently taking. This includes both prescribed and over-the-counter substances.

6. Ask Questions: Don't hesitate to ask questions about the herbal remedies recommended to you, their potential benefits, possible side effects, and interactions with medications. A good professional will be willing to address your concerns and provide clear answers.

7. Understand Risks and Benefits: Seek to understand both the potential benefits and risks associated with the herbal remedies suggested. Consider the evidence supporting their use and how they may interact with your individual health conditions.

8. Follow Recommendations: If you decide to use herbal remedies based on the professional's advice, follow their recommendations regarding dosages, administration methods, and duration of use.

9. Monitor Progress: Keep track of how herbal remedies affect your health over time. If you experience any adverse effects or concerns, report them to the healthcare professional or herbalist.

10. Stay Engaged: Maintain regular follow-ups with the professional, especially if you are using herbal remedies for ongoing health issues. Regular check-ins can help monitor your

progress and make any necessary adjustments to your
treatment plan.

11. Be Patient: Herbal remedies may take time to show their
effects, especially for chronic health conditions. Be patient and
committed to the treatment plan.

Remember, healthcare professionals and herbalists are there to help
you achieve optimal health. By following these best practices, you can
have a productive and positive experience during your consultations and
make informed decisions about using herbal remedies to support your
well-being.

Conclusion

"A Comprehensive Guide to Medicinal Plants and Their Uses" provides you with valuable knowledge about the wonderful world of herbal medicine. By incorporating these natural remedies into your lifestyle, you can benefit from their healing properties and promote overall well-being. However, it is essential to remember that while medicinal plants can be powerful allies, seeking advice from qualified healthcare professionals is crucial for proper diagnosis and treatment. Embrace the ancient wisdom of herbal medicine while respecting the importance of modern healthcare practices.